a cookbook for students

Visit us at: nosh4students.com

Published by:
InTRADE (GB) Ltd, 25 Greenway, Manor Park, Letchworth, Herts, SG63UG, UK
Phone 01462 637223, email: joymay@ntlworld.com

Author: Joy May

ISBN: 0-9543179-0-4

Printed by:
ACTSCo, Ltd. Chiang Mai, Thailand
(66-53) 960-290 email: actsco@loxinfo.co.th

Introduction

This recipe book was inspired by my son Ben. He left for University with virtually no ability to cook, apart from toasted ham sandwiches. He did, however, like to eat. He soon began to ring home to ask how to cook various things. I sent him a few index cards with recipes on them but they had no visual imagery to inspire him or for him to understand what the food should look like when finished. I searched for a good visual student cook book but could not find one, so I decided to produce one, not just for Ben but for other students like him. I hope that you enjoy these recipes.

The stars ****** are an indication of how easy the recipes are. One star is very quick and easy, the five stars are for you to try when you are a little more accomplished. Most of the food in the book is healthy and well balanced, but there is the odd, over indulgent one!

Approximately half the recipes are either vegetarian or have a vegetarian alternative. If you are a 'fish eating vegetarian' then there are plenty of recipes for you to use.

The recipes are planned so that you need the minimum of pans, dishes and utensils. A list of cooking equipment to take with you to University is on the next page.

Dedicated to Ben

Author
Joy May

Limited Utensils

These recipes have been written
so that you will be able to produce them
using just the following utensils

To measure:
mug (approx. 1/2 pint)
tablespoon, size mum serves with
desert spoon, one you eat cereal with
teaspoon

To prepare and cook with:
wooden spoon
chopping board
sharp knife
small pan with lid
medium sized pan with lid
frying pan
casserole dish with lid
flat roasting dish or metal non stick cooking tray
microwaveable plate

Good buying ideas

1. Look through the recipe book before you go to the supermarket and buy ingredients for specific recipes, this way you will not waste food or be frustrated that you don't have all the ingredients to complete a recipe. See pages 89 - 92 for sample menus and shopping lists.
2. Buy in 'bulk' when things are on offer in the supermarkets and store excess in your freezer drawer.
3. If you have access to a freezer or part of a freezer buy things like larger packets of frozen mince, chicken breasts or small chicken breast fillets, cubed meats, and fish fillets. This means that you will buy more than you need for one occasion, but it will cost much less in the long term.
4. Buy whole chickens and cook them, use the meat for one meal and then freeze the rest in portions. Use it later for sandwiches, baked potatoes, salads, risottos. Much cheaper than buying ready cooked chicken.
5. Keep things in stock like pasta, rice, flour, corn flour, salt and pepper.
6. Basic things to liven-up boring food are: Worcestershire Sauce, Soy Sauce, a few freeze-dried herbs (basil, parsley, mixed herbs), stock cubes, pilau rice cubes, tomato sauce, tomato puree, and garlic.
7. Curry paste - much better than curry powder, use it in all sorts of things, liven up baked beans for instance!
8. Spare loaf of bread and pint of milk in the freezer - don't freeze milk in glass bottles, use the plastic bottles or cartons.
9. Always make sure that when you visit home you return to Uni having creamed off any excess from mum's cupboards!

What do I do If???????

I don't have a microwave – To reheat a plate of food cover the plate with a pan lid or some foil. Place over a pan of boiling water and cook for 10 - 15 minutes.

To defrost food – Wait!! Do not try to speed things up by placing the food in boiling water, especially things like chicken. Frozen mince is fine to use in many of the recipes in this book: just add it straight from the packet and put the rest of the pack back in the freezer.

I don't have a lid for the casserole – use some foil, tear off enough to wrap around the edges of the dish and mold it to the dish with your hands.

I don't have a pastry brush – Use your fingers or a spoon.

I don't have a garlic press – Peel the garlic and put on a board. Put a chopping knife flat on the garlic and the flat base of the palm of your hand on top, press down hard and the skin will come off easily, then chop the garlic finely.

Everything I cook in the oven is burnt! – It could be that if you have an older oven the thermostat is not working quite as well as it should. Don't give up, just adjust by lowering the temperature you set it to.

Everything I cook in the oven is undercooked! – Oven temperatures vary, check whether you have a Centigrade or Fahrenheit oven, then check the temperature on the recipe. If you have followed the instructions correctly it could be that your oven thermostat is old, so increase the temperature slightly.

If everything you cook on top of the cooker is burnt – either you need to keep the heat turned down or you just need to keep an eye on things. You can't go off and ring your mates whilst trying to cook successfully.

How long can I keep this before it kills me?

RAW MEAT - 1 day in the fridge BACON - 2 to 3 days in the fridge

COOKED MEAT - 3 days maximum in the fridge

EGGS – 2 to 3 weeks

MILK - 2 days once opened. Unopened it should keep until the best before date, but needs to be in the fridge.

BUTTER and MARGARINE SPREADS - 2 to 3 weeks

CHEESE - 1 week once opened, 2 weeks unopened, keep cheese wrapped with cling film or it will go dry and horrid. Green mold on cheese, other than the blue varieties, means that it is best thrown away.

VEGETABLES - vary, some keep better in the fridge, others out.

ONIONS and POTATOES – keep for about one week, best out of the fridge and in a dark place. Once potatoes have gone green they are not very good for you!

GREEN VEGETABLES - keep better in the fridge as do carrots, parsnips etc.

SALAD, LETTUCE, CUCUMBER, TOMATOES, PEPPERS etc - keep in the fridge up to a week. Keep lettuce covered.

Keep everything covered in the fridge, this helps things keep better and rules out cross contamination if you share a fridge with someone who leaves disgusting things in there! Cling film is a wonderful and inexpensive invention.

Don't keep tins in the fridge: once opened the tin will begin to make the food taste of metal and not do you much good.

Basic Hygiene in the Kitchen

Keep your dishcloth and tea towels clean!

Clean your chopping board after cutting raw meat!

Wash up now and then!!???!

Take care when reheating food that you heat it thoroughly.

Vegetables

Depending on your taste, you do not always need to peel veggies. Washing them is a good idea. Larger things like potatoes and carrots need to be cut into pieces before cooking, broccoli broken into 'small trees' and so on.

Boiled vegetables

Generally most vegetables need to be cooked in enough water to cover them. Bring the water to the boil, once boiling add the vegetables and a little salt and simmer gently with the lid on the pan. If you keep the source of the heat low, not only will you preserve a little more nutrition in the vegetables, but you will also avoid burnt pans and very mucky cookers where the pans have boiled over.

Here are some approximate cooking times

Potatoes ~ 15 minutes
Broccoli ~ 5 minutes, boiling gently.
Green beans ~ 5 - 10 minutes
Carrots ~ 10 - 15 minutes
Cauliflower ~ 10 minutes
Spinach ~ 1 - 2 minutes, just enough to make the leaves wilt. You will only need a little water in the bottom of the pan.
Swedes and Turnips ~ 20 - 25 minutes
Parsnips ~ 10 - 15 minutes
Leeks ~ 5 - 10 minutes
Cabbage ~ 5 - 10 minutes. Again you only need a little water, drain after cooking and add some butter and black pepper. Return to the pan and cook for another 2 minutes to dry the cabbage a little.

If You really want the fuss of mashed potatoes you will need to peel them first. Boil them as above: once they are cooked through, mash them, either with a fork or a potato masher whilst adding a little milk and butter.

Roast potatoes Brush the potatoes with cooking oil, sprinkle with salt and place on a baking dish or casserole dish. The potatoes should not be piled on top of each other. Cook in the oven at 190 or gas 8 for 45 minutes to an hour.

Baked Potatoes see page 18

How to cook pasta

There are innumerable kinds of Pasta to chose from in the shops, made from different ingredients. Most will have instructions on the packets as to how to cook them. Just in case you have lost the packet here are some general guidelines:

1. Spaghetti

For one person, depending on appetite, you need a bunch of spaghetti approximately the diameter of a 50p piece. Boil sufficient water in a pan to cover the spaghetti whilst cooking. Once the water is boiling lower the spaghetti sticks into the water. Once the ha that is in the water has softened slightly, push the other half in. Take care not to get you fingers in the water. Simmer for 8 - 10 minutes. Test to see if it is cooked. Drain the water off and add one teaspoon of butter or olive oil, mix around and this will stop the spaghetti sticking together.

2. Most other pastas

Again, boil enough water to cover the pasta. Once th water is boiling add the pasta. One mug of dried pas is plenty for one person with a very healthy appetite. Simmer for the appropriate time, drain and add butte or olive oil to prevent the pasta sticking together.

3. Cooking times

Tagliatelli, smaller pasta twists, small macaroni - approx 5 minutes

Riccioli, Tirali, Fusilli and thicker twists 8 - 11 minutes

Some varieties of pasta like penne may take as long as 15 minutes to cook.

Pasta is better slightly undercooked than overcooke

How to cook rice

There are many different types of rice to buy. I would recommend that you use basmati, it is slightly more expensive than long grain or quick cook rice, but has a much better flavor and texture than the cheaper varieties.

Rice for one person = ½ mug rice + 1 mug water. Knorr Pilau rice cubes (or other rice flavor cubes) transform rice from tasteless to yummy.

1. Using a pan with a lid, bring the water to the boil, add the flavor cube and stir until it has dissolved.

2. Add the rice and stir, bring back to the boil. Once boiling turn down the heat to very low so that the rice simmers gently. Put the lid on the pan and cook for approximately 15 minutes. Do not stir whilst the rice is cooking or you will make it sticky. The rice should be cooked once the water has disappeared. Don't keep lifting the lid, as during the last part of the cooking time the rice is steaming.

3. Test the rice after the 15 minutes. If the rice is still too crunchy and the water has all gone then you have boiled it too quickly. Add a little more water, replace the lid and cook for another 5 minutes.

To make egg fried rice

. Cook the rice as above using a pilau rice cube.

. Using one egg per quantity of rice, beat the egg in a mug. Heat some butter or oil in a frying pan. Pour the egg into the pan and allow it to spread all over the base. Cook until the egg is set, remove from the pan and cut the egg up into strips.

. Using the same frying pan add a little more oil and some finely chopped onion (onion per person), fry until the onion is browned.

. If the pan is large enough for the quantity of rice you have cooked add the rice and egg to the onions and stir well. If you have a larger quantity then add the onions and the egg to the rice pan.

'Cook in Sauces'

There are many 'cook in sauces' on the market and they are very easy to use, but are, of course, much more expensive than making sauces from basic ingredients. It is good to get mum to buy you a few when you come back to Uni, they make li easier, save them for when you are really pressed for time and need a good meal. Here are some ideas to help you to use them.

Most 'economy meats', i.e. chicken thighs and legs, stewing meats etc need to cook for a long time if they are to be edible. You can cook them in the sauces but you will need to add extra liquid as the sauces will dry up during the cooking time. Add the "cook in sauce" to the chicken thighs, for example, but add another $\frac{1}{2}$ jar of water, mix well and cook in a covered dish in the oven for $1\frac{1}{2}$ hours with the heat at 170 C/Reg 6. It is best to take the skins off chicken thighs as they contain a lot of fat and will make the dish very greasy if they are not removed. Stewing meats, lamb or beef will take the same length of time to cook. Chicken legs will cook at the same temperature but only need 45 minutes to 1 hour to cook, depending on how tender you like them.

If you are using chicken breasts or small chicken breast fillets cut the meat into bite-size chunks and fry in a little oil or butter for approximately 4 - 5 minutes. Once the meat is cooked through add the "cook in sauce" and once boiling simmer for a further 2 - 3 minutes.

If you are using mince fry in a little oil. Once the mince is no longer pink add the "cook in sauce", bring to the boil and then simmer for 2 - 3 minutes.

If you are using a Bolognese sauce fry the mince in a little oil first and then add the sauce. You can either eat this with spaghetti or pasta or add to dry pasta and bake in the oven for 20 - 25 minutes 180 C/Reg 7

If you have left-over cooked meat; for example, if you have cooked a chicken, simply add to the sauce and bring to the boil, simmer for 4 - 5 minutes to make sure that the meat is properly reheated.

If all you have left in your freezer or fridge are sausages you can use these with "cook in sauces", brown them well and make sure they are cooked through before adding the sauce.

If you want to eat vegetarian food add a "cook in sauce" to dry pasta and cook in the oven, uncovered for 20 - 25 minutes, 180 C/Reg 7. If you are using a bolognese type sauce grate some cheese on the top, this will add extra flavour. Vegetarians can use "cook in sauces" with cooked vegetables, follow the instructions for Vegetable Bake on page 61. Adding the sauce to raw vegetables will not work well.

Jacket Potatoes

1. Use medium or large potatoes. Always slit the skin with a knife before baking or it may explode in the oven or the microwave.
2. Either bake in the oven, 200 C/gas 9 for 1 hour or in a microwave for 7 - 10 minutes, depending on how large the potato is.
3. When the potato is cooked cut it open and add any of the following suggestions, together with a little butter to moisten:

Baked beans
Cheese
Tuna and Mayonnaise
Cottage cheese, on it's own or with shrimps, tuna, ham, tomatoes, peppers etc.
Cooked chicken and mayonnaise, you can add a little mustard to the mayonnaise or ½ teaspoon curry paste
Chili con carne, recipe page 48 or you could buy a tin.
Smoked mackerel, take the skin off and break up slightly, add some mayonnaise
Crispy bacon and hard boiled eggs, chopped up together
Natural Yoghourt, pepper, sweet corn, chili powder
Natural yoghourt, sliced mushrooms, 1 teaspoon tomato puree, 1 teaspoon mild curry paste

Jacket potatoes are good served with a little salad, lettuce, tomatoes, cucumber and spring onions.

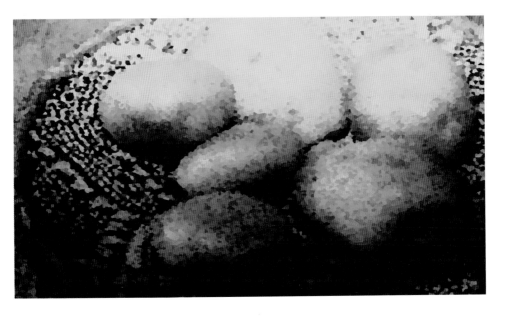

Bread

Eggie Bread

1. Break an egg into a mug and beat with a fork. Turn out onto a plate.
2. Dip the bread into the egg and let the bread soak up the egg on both sides.
3. Put 2 teaspoons of butter in a frying pan and heat until the butter starts to bubble. Add the bread and cook gently until both sides are browned.
4. Serve with beans and HP or tomato sauce.
5. You can make this sweet by adding a dessert spoon of sugar to the egg at the beginning.

Cinnamon Toast

1. Toast bread very lightly on both sides and butter on one side.
2. Make a mixture of 1 teaspoon cinnamon and 3 teaspoon sugar and sprinkle on top of the toast.
3. Put it back under the grill and heat until the sugar has dissolved.
4. Americans eat this with boiled eggs for breakfast. Brits eat it as a snack.

Bread and butter pudding

If you have a large amount of bread left over, slice and butter it, arrange it in a casserole dish, sprinkle with 3 - 4 dessert spoons of sugar. You can add currants and/or sprinkle on a teaspoon of cinnamon if you have it. Beat 2 or 3 eggs in a bowl and add a mug of milk, pour over the bread.
Place in the oven at 180 C for 30 - 35 mins, the top should be browned.

French Toast

Butter the bread before toasting. Toast the butter side first and then the reverse side.

Garlic Bread

This works best with bread sticks but you can do the same with other breads; for example, buns.

1. Take 3 large cloves of garlic, peel and crush them, mix well with 2 tablespoons butter. You can add 1 teaspoon of freeze dried chives or parsley, if you wish.
2. Make diagonal cuts in the bread stick, ensuring that you don't cut right through. Push the butter into the cuts.
3. Wrap the bread stick in foil and place on a baking sheet or oven-proof dish. Cook for 6 - 7 minutes at 220 or Gas 9

Fried bread

Simply heat some oil or butter in a frying pan, dip the bread in both sides to absorb the oil evenly, then fry on each side for approximately 2 minutes or until browned.

Sandwiches

Ideas for fillings

Bacon (plus brown sauce).
Bacon (cooked hot and crisp) and banana (not cooked).
Honey and banana.
Scrambled eggs (can add some cheese to egg whilst cooking, see page 15).
Cottage cheese or cream cheese, both great with jam or honey and bananas.
Cottage cheese with tomatoes or cucumber, remember to season well.
Cream cheese with tomato, ham.
Egg mayonnaise - hard boiled eggs, chopped and mixed with mayo, season well.
Salmon and cucumber - can add mayonnaise.
Tuna, hard boiled egg, spring onion and mayonnaise.
Cheese and tomato.

Ham and cheese	Fried egg
Cheese and pickle	Marmite!
Cheese and Jam, raspberry works well	Peanut butter and jam or marmalade
Boiled egg and tomato	peanut butter and honey and/or bananas
bacon and mayonnaise	chicken and mayonnaise with lettuce
Sausages and Brown Sauce	bacon lettuce and tomato

Toasted sandwiches

Your mum may have an old sandwich toaster up in the loft or out in the garage. Seek it out and take it with you to Uni. The idea of the sandwich toaster was to make the sandwich with the butter side of the bread on the outside, this makes the bread more tasty on the toasted side. If you make toasted sandwiches under the grill put the buttered side on the inside or the butter will just melt and drip off. You can use all the above fillings in toasted sandwiches apart from the ones containing lettuce or cucumber

Eggs

Poach

1. Using a small pan or frying pan, half fill with water and add a good pinch of salt. Bring to the boil, then turn down until the water is only just moving.
2. Break the egg into a mug or cup, gently pour into water. Do not stir or turn the heat up, just let it cook gently. It will take 2 - 4 minutes, depending on the size of the egg.
3. Once the egg has gone opaque, gently lift out with a fish slice and let the water drain from it.
4. Great with beans on toast, tomato sauce or HP.

Scramble

1. Using a small milk pan, preferably non stick, add 2 teaspoons butter, heat gently until the butter bubbles.
2. Break the egg into the pan and add salt and pepper. Stir slowly, breaking up the egg yolk.
3. When the egg is almost set take off the heat. The egg will continue to cook in it's own heat. If you cook it too long it will become rubbery.
4. You can add grated cheese and/or chopped tomatoes half way through the cooking.

Fry

Not the healthiest way to eat eggs but if you must (they make a great supper snack as fried egg butties)

1. Heat 2 teaspoons butter in the frying pan until the butter just bubbles.
2. Break the egg into a mug and then gently pour into the frying pan.
3. Cook on medium heat until the egg is set.
4. Using a fish slice turn the egg over half-way through cooking if you want 'easy over' or a hard yolk.

Boil

1. Using a small pan fill 3/5 full with water and bring to the boil.
2. Lower the egg into the pan on a spoon.
3. Simmer briskly for 3 minutes for a very runny egg. 5 minutes and you will still be able to dip your soldiers in the runny yolk. 12 minutes and it will be hard boiled.

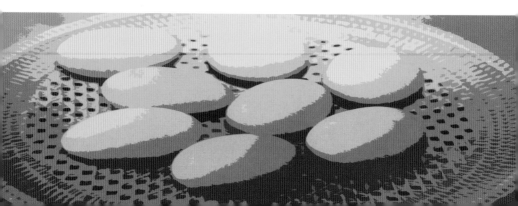

Omelettes

Instructions for a basic omelette

1. Put two or three eggs in a mug and beat well with a fork, add two tablespoons of water.
2. Switch on the grill to full heat to warm up.
3. Melt about a dessert spoon of butter in the frying pan. Once it begins to 'bubble' pour the egg mixture into the pan.
4. As it sets on the bottom of the pan gently move the set egg with fish slice and allow the runny egg to take it's place. Do this with two or three sweeping movements, don't stir or you will get scrambled egg. Repeat this process once more.
5. While there is still a little runny egg on the top add whatever filling you want, top with cheese (not essential) and place the frying pan under the hot grill. Watch carefully, the omelette should rise. Once it is browned on the top remove from the grill and turn out onto a plate. Serve with salad, garlic bread or baked potatoes.

Suggested fillings - cheese, tomato, mushrooms, fried onions, crispy grilled bacon cut into pieces, cooked chicken, ham or any combination of these ingredients.

Sweet omelettes - add fruit (strawberries, raspberries or blackcurrants are the best kind of fruit), sugar, cinnamon or jam.

Pancakes

Pancakes are easy to make and are good fun when you have friends around. Just make sure you are not the only one standing cooking them. Tossing them is always fun, catching them not guaranteed.

Recipe

Makes about 6.

2 eggs
6 tablespoons plain flour
Milk
Trex or white flora to fry (you can use oil but a lard type is best)

1. Beat the eggs and flour together in a bowl or jug, gradually add the milk, making sure there are no lumps. The mixture should be as thin as single cream, quite thin, but not as thin as milk.
2. Heat about ½" cube of lard in a frying pan, when the fat begins to smoke a little pour approximately 2 tablespoons of the mixture into the pan, tip the pan around so that the mixture spreads over the surface of the pan. Let the mixture cook for about 1 minute.
3. Gently lift the edge of the pancake to see if it is browned. Once browned turn the pancake with a fish slice or toss and then cook the other side.

Serve with lemon juice and sugar, undiluted squashes, any kind of ice cream, maple syrup, golden syrup, fruit such as strawberries, jam or ice cream sauces.

You can make savoury pancakes. Use the same method as above, make fillings such as tuna and mayonnaise, cottage cheese and tomato, chicken and ham in a cheese sauce (see page 19).

QUICK CHEESE SAUCE ★

Preparation and cooking time 10 - 15 minutes
for 1   Vegetarian

This is a simple useful and versatile basic sauce.

1 mug grated cheese
1 tablespoon flour
1 teaspoon butter
1 mug milk
⅛ teaspoon paprika
salt and pepper

1. Put the grated cheese into a saucepan, add the flour, salt and pepper and paprika and stir well.
2. Add the milk and bring to the boil, stirring all the time, the sauce should thicken.

Double this quantity for vegetable bake and cauliflower cheese.

ITALIAN SOUP ★

Preparation and cooking time 20 minutes
Vegetarian   for 2 - 3

The ingredients for this soup may seem a little complicated, don't worry if you don't have them all: the celery and the spinach can be left out if you wish.

1 small potato, diced
1 carrot diced
1 onion chopped
3 teaspoons butter
$\frac{1}{2}$ red pepper
1 - 2 celery sticks
14 oz/400g tin of tomatoes
2 cloves garlic crushed

3 mugs water
1 chicken stock cube
2 pieces frozen spinach
1 teaspoon freeze dried basil
$\frac{1}{4}$ cup small macaroni
1 tablespoon tomato puree
salt and pepper

1. Melt butter in saucepan add onions, potato, carrot, pepper, celery and garlic and cook for 2 minutes, stirring well.
2. Add the tin of tomatoes, tomato puree, water and stock cube, bring to the boil. Cook for 10 minutes then add the macaroni and cook for a further 4 minutes.
3. Add the spinach and the basil and season well.

VEGETABLE SOUP ★

Preparation and cooking time 20 minutes.   vegetarian   for 1

This is a good easy soup for a winter day, the ingredients listed make a good combination but you can use whatever vegetables you have to hand.

1 small potato cut into cubes
1 medium sized carrot peeled and sliced
1 stick of celery cut into pieces
½ medium onion chopped
pieces of ham (optional)
½ vegetable or chicken stock cube

1 ½ mugs water
¼ mug frozen peas
1 teaspoon butter
1 teaspoon flour
salt and pepper

1. Fry the onion in the butter.
2. Add the potatoes and carrots and cook for about 30 seconds.
3. Add flour and mix in with the vegetables.
4. Add the water and stock and bring to the boil, simmer for 10 minutes or until the vegetables are cooked.
5. Add the celery and the peas, cook for 2 minutes.
6. Add the pieces of ham and cook for 1 minute.
7. Serve with bread.

MULLIGATAWNY SOUP ★

Preparation time 10 minutes, cooking time 20 minutes.
for 2 - 3

This is more of a stew than a soup, very substantial. If you reheat this soup the
next day make sure that it boils and then simmers slowly for about 3 - 4 minutes
Reheat in a microwave for 1 minute on a high setting.

1 teaspoon cooking oil
½ onion, chopped
1 carrot, peeled and sliced
1 stick celery cut into small pieces
1 eating apple cut into chunks
2 - 3 teaspoons curry paste (mild)
4 small chicken breast fillets (raw) cut into small pieces
salt and pepper

½ teaspoon ground coriander
3 mugs water
1 chicken stock cube
14oz/400g tin of chopped tomatoes
¼ cup long grain rice

1. Fry the onion, carrot and celery.
2. Add the rest of the ingredients and bring to the boil. Simmer for 20 minutes,
stirring occasionally.

SAUSAGE SOUP ★★

Preparation and cooking time 15 – 20 minutes   For 1

This soup is inexpensive, easy to cook, tasty and filling. Reheating sausages is never a good idea so it is best to make only as much as you will eat at one time, you can always make more and share it.

4 small or 2 large sausages, cooked (spicy sausages work well with this recipe).
1 small onion, chopped
1 teaspoon butter
3 teaspoons Worcestershire sauce
$\frac{1}{4}$ mug pasta, tagliatelli, macaroni, small twists
1 beef stock cube
small tin baked beans
salt and pepper
1 $\frac{1}{2}$ mugs water

1. Fry the onion in butter.
2. Add the water, stock cube and pasta, bring to the boil and simmer gently for 4 - 5 minutes.
3. While the pasta is simmering cook the sausages if not already cooked.
5. Add the sausages, beans and Worcestershire sauce cook for 2 minutes.

Preparation and cooking time approximately 30 minutes
Vegetarian   for 2

This is a meal for when you are cold and hungry, it's tasty, inexpensive and filling. Keep some suet in the fridge as you can use it to make pie crusts, see recipe on page 32 (Lamb Cobbler)

1 large carrot, peeled and sliced
1 large onion, chopped.
1 large potato, cut into pieces
14 oz tin chopped tomatoes
1 ½ mugs water
1 beef or vegetable stock cube
2 teaspoons butter to fry
3 - 4 mushrooms sliced
1 teaspoon curry paste, more if you like it hot.

Salt and pepper
1 teaspoon coriander leaves (freeze dried)
½ mug suet
1 mug self raising flour, plain won't work, the dumplings will be solid
1 egg + water to mix

1. Fry the onions in the butter, add potatoes and carrots, cook for 30 seconds.
2. Add the tin of tomatoes, stock cube, curry paste water and mushrooms, bring to the boil and leave to simmer gently while you make the dumplings.
3. In a bowl, a cereal bowl will do, mix together the flour suet, salt and coriander.
4. In a mug, beat the egg and a little water, add to the flour mixture and stir around, add sufficient egg and water to form a soft ball of dough, not too wet.
5. Put some flour onto a board or plate, turn the mixture out onto it, squeeze gently to form a ball, cut into 8 pieces, forming each one into a ball.
6. Add these to the simmering soup and cook gently for 10 - 15 minutes. If you have a lid put it on the pan and the dumplings will cook quicker.

CHICKEN AND SWEETCORN SOUP ★★

Preparation and cooking time 10 minutes
for 1

This soup is more substantial and nutritious than the Chinese take-away versions, it is just as tasty and will form a meal in itself.

1 teaspoon butter
1 teaspoon cornflour
1 chicken stock cube
1 mug water
1 egg

1 teaspoon soy sauce
¼ tin sweetcorn
salt and pepper
1 teaspoon freeze dried chives

3 spring onions, chopped, you could use an ordinary onion
2 small pieces uncooked chicken breast fillet cut into small pieces

1. Fry the onions in the butter until soft.
2. Add the water, soy sauce and stock cube.
3. Add the chicken (you must use chicken breast or the meat will not cook properly) and sweetcorn, cook until the chicken is no longer pink, approximately 2 - 3 minutes.
4. Mix the cornflour with a little water in a mug. Add to the soup, stirring well until it comes back to the boil and thickens, don't let the soup boil for a long time.
5. Beat the egg in a mug and pour into the soup, leave until the egg begins to set and then stir once only, this way the egg will stay together.
6. Cook until the egg goes white.   Add salt and pepper.

ROAST POTATOES AND SAUSAGES ★

Preparation time 5 minutes, cooking time 1 hour.

vegetarian option   for 2

Very quick and simple way to get delicious roast potatoes, an inexpensive taste of home.

6 - 8 frozen sausages, beef, pork or vegetarian
4 - 6 potatoes
1 tablespoon cooking oil
1 onion
salt and pepper

1. Wash potatoes and cut into large wedges, peel the onion and cut into 6.
2. Oil the casserole dish or baking tray and place the potatoes, sausages and onions in it, brush everything with the oil and season well with salt and pepper.
3. Put in the oven set at 180 C/Reg 7 for 30 minutes. Take out of the oven and carefully turn things over so that they brown on the other side. Cook for a further 20 - 30 minutes or until everything is browned.
4. Serve with baked beans.

EASY BEEF STROGANOFF ★★★

Preparation time 15 - 20 minutes, cooking time 1 hour 30 minutes
for 2

Slightly more pricey dish but delicious, everything but the wine is essential in this dish for it to taste right.

½ x 500g pack of cubed stewing beef or beef cut into thin strips
1 onion, chopped
1 tablespoon flour
½ pint yoghourt or soured cream
2 teaspoons freeze dried basil or parsley
1 desert spoon dijon mustard
glass white wine (optional)
2 cloves garlic, crushed

1 desert spoon cooking oil
1 beef stock cube
1 mug water
3 - 4 mushrooms
¼ teaspoon paprika
salt and pepper

1. Fry the onion in the oil.
2. Add the meat and cook on a medium heat until the meat is slightly browned, or until the outsides of the cubes are no longer pink.
3. Add the flour and stir well. Add the water, stock cube, garlic, mustard and mushrooms and bring to the boil.
4. Simmer with a lid on the pan for 1 ½ hours.
6. Remove from the heat and add the yoghourt and parsley.
7. Serve with rice and green vegetables, broccoli, green beans etc.

Preparation and cooking time 15 - 20 minutes
for 1
This makes a quick and filling snack, you could keep most of the ingredients in
your store cupboard.

Pasta (tagliatelli, 2 'bunches')	1 desert spoon flour
2 slices of ham	1 hard boiled egg
1 onion, chopped	$\frac{1}{2}$ mug milk + $\frac{1}{2}$ mug cream/milk
1 teaspoon butter	$\frac{1}{2}$ teaspoon freeze dried basil
3 - 4 mushrooms	salt and pepper

1. Put pasta on to boil (See page 10).
2. Fry onion in the butter.
3. Add the flour and stir well, cook for 30 seconds.
4. Take off the heat and add the milk and cream, stir well and return to the heat, the mixture should thicken slightly.
5. Add the mushrooms, ham and basil and cook for 1 minute.
6. Cut the hard boiled egg into 4 and add, don't stir too much or the egg will break up.
7. Drain the pasta, put on serving plate and pour the ham mixture over.

Preparation time 10 minutes, cooking time 50 minutes.
Vegetarian option   For 2

This dish is easy to prepare and will make enough for two meals, it is fine microwaved the next day.

½ x 500g pack of frozen beef, lamb or Quorn mince
1 onion sliced
1x 14oz/400g tin baked beans
1 teaspoon butter
4 - 5 potatoes, washed and sliced
2 teaspoons Worcestershire sauce
1 stock cube, beef, lamb or vegetable according to meat.

1. Fry the onion in the butter until soft.
2. Add the mince or Quorn and cook until the mince is no longer pink, or Quorn heated through.
3. Add stock cube, but no water, the cube will dissolve in the meat mixture.
4. Add the tin of beans and Worcestershire sauce and pour into a casserole dish.
5. Place the sliced potatoes on top of the meat in layers and cook for 50 minutes at 180 C/Reg 7.

LASAGNA ★★★★★

Preparation time 25 minutes, cooking time 25 minutes
vegetarian option   for 4

Although this dish is a little complicated it is not impossible for an inexperienced cook. Once you have mastered Spaghetti Bolognese and the quick cheese sauce try this recipe when you have a few friends around.

Bolognese Sauce
1 x 500g pack of minced beef, lamb or Quorn
14 oz /400g tin chopped tomatoes
1 onion, chopped
1 dessert spoon cooking oil
2 cloves garlic, crushed
1 tablespoon tomato puree
1 teaspoon mixed herbs
salt and pepper

Quick Cheese sauce
2 mugs grated cheese
2 tablespoons flour
2 mugs milk
½ teaspoon paprika
½ teaspoon nutmeg
salt and pepper

1 x 250g packet of lasagna strips

1. Make the cheese sauce (see page 19).
2. Make the Bolognese sauce (see page 31).
3. Put a layer of Bolognese sauce at the bottom of the casserole dish, an oblong dish is easiest, but if you only have a round one break up the pasta strips to fit.
4. Next put a layer of cheese sauce, pasta strips, rest of the Bolognese sauce, more pasta strips and then the rest of the cheese sauce and finally top with some grated cheese.
6. Cook for 25 minutes at 180 C/Reg 7.
6. Serve with salad or garlic bread.

Preparation and cooking time 20 minutes   for 2

vegetarian option

'Spag Bol' is a must to master. If you cook enough sauce for two you can either share it with a flat mate or the next day add either curry paste or chili and eat with rice or baked potatoes.

½ x 500g packet of frozen mince, beef, lamb or Quorn

14 oz/400g tin chopped tomatoes

1 onion, chopped

1 teaspoon cooking oil

2 cloves garlic

1 tablespoon tomato puree

1 teaspoon sugar

1 teaspoon freeze dried mixed herbs

1 glass red wine (if available)

4 - 5 mushroom, sliced (optional)

salt and pepper

Spaghetti

1. Fry the onion in the oil until soft.
2. Add the mince and cook until the meat is no longer pink.
3. Add the tin of tomatoes, tomato puree, mushrooms garlic, sugar and wine. Bring to boil and simmer gently for 10 minutes. Add the herbs one minute before the end of the cooking time and season well with salt and pepper.
4. Put spaghetti on to cook. (see page 10 for how much and how to cook)
5. Drain the pasta, add a little butter or olive oil to stop it sticking together. Serve on plate with Bolognese sauce on the top.
6. Serve with Parmesan cheese and green salad.

LAMB COBBLER ★★★

Preparation time 20 minutes, cooking time 30 minutes   for 2
vegetarian option
Winter warmer, this recipe is a little fiddly but is inexpensive and filling. If you
like the topping it can be used instead of potatoes with other recipes such as
Shepherds pie or Monday Pie.

½ x 500g packet of frozen mince, lamb or Quorn
1 onion
1 dessert spoon cooking oil
14 oz/400g tin chopped tomatoes
1 teaspoon mixed herbs

1 tablespoon tomato puree
½ cup water
salt and pepper

Scone topping
1 mug self raising flour
½ mug suet
½ mug water
pinch salt
1 teaspoon freeze dried basil
or coriander

1. Fry the onion in the oil until soft.
2. Add the mince and cook until the meat is no longer pink.
3. Add the tomatoes, herbs, salt and pepper and tomato puree, stir well and simmer
for 5 minutes.
4. Transfer to a casserole dish.
5. To make the dumpling top - put flour, suet, salt and herbs in a dish and stir well. Add
the water until it makes a soft ball.
6. Put some flour onto a board or plate, turn out the mixture and form a ball.
7. Cut into six pieces and form each into a ball.
8. Gently place them on the top of the meat mixture, brush the top with beaten egg or
milk to help it brown. If you do not have a pastry brush use your fingers!
9. Bake for 25 - 30 minutes or until the crust is browned.

LANCASHIRE HOT POT ★★

Preparation time 5 - 10 minutes, cooking time 1 to 1 ½ hours
for 2

This is a very simple, tasty dish, quick to make and gives time for a little work while it cooks???!!

½ - ¾ x 500g pack of cubed lamb, you could use lamb mince
2 onions, cut into 6
2 - 3 potatoes
2 carrots
3 cloves of garlic, 1 lamb stock cube
2 mugs water
salt and pepper
2 tablespoons flour
1 desert spoon cooking oil

1. Fry the onions on a high heat until they brown slightly, add the meat and cook until the outside is no longer pink.
2. Add the flour and stir well.
3. Add the water and the stock cube, bring to the boil, the liquid should thicken.
4. Cut the carrots and potatoes into chunks and add to the mixture.
5. Transfer to a casserole dish with a lid and cook for 1- ½ hour at 180 C/Reg 7, if you use lamb mince you will only need to cook for 1 hour.

BEEFY MINCE AND PASTA BAKE

Preparation time 5 - 10 minutes, cooking time 20 - 25 minutes
for 2 - 3   vegetarian option

Very simple to make, good dish to make and share with flat mates, is ok reheated
in the microwave but best eaten straight away.

1 x 14oz/400g tin of Campbell's condensed tomato soup (undiluted)
¾ packet x 500g frozen mince or Quorn
1 beef/vegetable stock cube
1 ½ mugs pasta
1 onion, chopped
1 teaspoon butter

½ mug grated cheese
2 cloves garlic, crushed
1 teaspoon freeze dried basil
salt and pepper

1. Cook the pasta, (see page 10)
2. Fry the onion in the butter until soft.
3. Add the mince and cook until no longer pink.
4. Add the stock cube, tomato soup , herbs and salt and pepper.
5. Drain the pasta well and add to the meat mixture. Transfer to a casserole dish.
6. Top with grated cheese and cook at 200 C/Reg 8 for 20 - 25 minutes, or until the top
is browned.

SPICY RISOTTO ★★

Preparation and cooking time 20 minutes   for 1
vegetarian option

This is a tasty dish, if you like hot food you can add more curry paste.
It reheats well,
so making double
quantity is a
good idea.

½ mug rice
1 mug water
½ pilau rice cube
¼ - ⅓ x 500g packet of lamb, beef or Quorn mince
1 small onion, chopped
2 mushrooms, sliced
1 clove garlic, crushed
½ lamb or vegetable stock cube
¼ mug water

1 teaspoon coriander leaves
2 teaspoons mild curry paste
1 teaspoon butter
salt and pepper

1. Cook rice, with pilau rice cube see page 11.
2. Fry the onion in the butter until the onions are soft.
3. Add the mince and cook until it is no longer pink.
4. Add the stock, mushrooms, garlic and a little water, bring to the boil and simmer for
5 minutes or so until all the liquid has gone.
5. When the liquid has gone from the rice and it is cooked transfer it to the meat mixture,
add salt and pepper and the coriander leaves. Serve with some salad.

MINCE HOT POT ★★

Preparation time 15 minutes, cooking time 45 - 50 minutes.
for 2   vegetarian optiont
With this dish you get yummy roasted potatoes on top of tasty meat sauce. It is
great microwaved the next day, so one cooking effort will give you two days
meals.

½ x 500g packet of lamb, beef or Quorn mince.
1 onion, chopped
3 - 4 mushrooms, sliced
14oz/400g tin of chopped tomatoes
1 tablespoon tomato puree
oil to fry
4 - 5 thinly sliced potatoes
1 teaspoon freeze dried basil
1 stock cube, beef, lamb or vegetable.

1. Fry the onion in the oil until soft.
2.. Add the mince and cook until no longer pink.
3. Add the tomatoes, mushrooms, tomato puree and stock cube, bring to the boil and then
transfer into a casserole dish.
4. Arrange the sliced , uncooked potatoes on the top in layers and brush the top with oil:
fingers will work if you don't have a pastry brush.
5. Cook for 45 - 50 minutes at 180 C/Reg 7, the potatoes should be browned on top.

Preparation time 10 minutes   for 1

Quick, easy, inexpensive lunch snack. You can replace the gammon with bacon or cooked ham

1 teaspoon butter
1 small onion, chopped
1 clove garlic, crushed
½ mug pasta
1 medium slice of gammon cut into pieces
2 mushrooms
8oz / 200g tin chopped tomatoes
1 teaspoon tomato puree
½ teaspoon freeze dried mixed herbs
Parmesan cheese (optional)
pepper

1. Cook pasta (see page 10)
2. Fry onions and and the chopped gammon.
3. Add mushrooms and garlic and cook for 1 minute.
4. Add the tomatoes and herbs, simmer for 2 - 3 minutes, season with pepper, you will not need salt as the bacon or ham will be salty enough.
6. Drain the pasta and add a small amount of butter or olive oil to stop the pasta sticking together.
7. Mix the sauce and pasta together, sprinkle with Parmesan if you wish.

POTATO WEDGES AND DIPS ★★

Preparation time 5 minutes, cooking time 25 minutes   Vegetarian

This is excellent party, or video night food, easy to make, almost like mums' chips

Wedges

2 medium potatoes per person
cooking oil
salt and pepper.

1. Cut the potatoes in half length ways, cutting each half into approximately 6 pieces each, producing thin 'wedges'.
2. Oil a baking tray, (flat tin) you can use a casserole dish if it is large enough.
3. Sprinkle more oil over the potatoes. Using your hands, toss the potatoes in the oil making sure that every piece of potato is covered in oil. Drain off any excess, if you have too much oil the potatoes will not be crisp. Separate the wedges leaving all the surfaces open to brown.
4. Season well with salt and pepper.
5. Cook for 25 - 30 minutes in a hot oven, 220 C/Reg 9 until potatoes are crisp and browned.

You can buy different flavourings in the supermarket for potato wedges, here are a few cheaper variations. Fill a mug ¼ full with oil and mix well with any of the following ingredients, crushed garlic , freeze dried herbs, paprika (don't use too much as it is very hot) small quantities of curry powder or finely grated cheese.

38

Preparation time 5 - 10 minutes.   Each of these dip recipes will serve 3 people

You can buy packets of dips in the supermarket. Here are a few ideas which are slightly less expensive and you can make them whilst the wedges are cooking.

1. Small carton of soured cream with ½ mug finely grated cheese and 1 teaspoon of mustard, season with salt and pepper.
2. Plain yoghourt mixed with ¼ cucumber chopped , ½ onion chopped, 1 teaspoon freeze dried mint.
3. Small carton soured cream or creme frais plus 2 cloves garlic, crushed + squeeze of lemon.
4. Small carton creme frais, plus 2 teaspoons tomato puree, 3 - 4 drops of tobasco sauce or 2 tablespoons chili sauce + 1 teaspoon sugar.
5. Small carton of plain yoghourt mixed with ½ mug mayonnaise together with the grated rind and juice of a lime, season with salt and pepper.
6. Small carton of soured cream plus 5 - 6 spring onions chopped + ½ mug finely grated cheese and salt and pepper.

These dips can be used if you have a party. Use carrot sticks, celery sticks, spicy crisps or cheese straws.

NOODLE OMELETTE ★★

Preparation and cooking time 10 - 15 minutes   for 2

Vegetarian options

This recipe is very versatile, if you are vegetarian you can add different cooked vegetables or tofu at stage 5; alternatively, you could add flaked tuna, ham cut into pieces, baked beans, crispy bacon, cooked chicken pieces and almost anything!

¼ x 250g packet of
egg noodles
1 onion, chopped
1 dessert spoon soy sauce
1 teaspoon freeze dried
4 eggs, beaten in a mug with 1 desert spoon water.

chives or mixed herbs
1 large tomato
½ mug grated cheese
butter to fry

1. Soak noodles in boiling water, leave for 4 minutes.
2. Using a frying pan, fry the onions in the butter, allowing them to brown a little.
3. Drain the noodles well and add to the frying pan, spreading them over the base of the pan. Allow them to fry a little, don't stir them.
4. Add the soy sauce and sprinkle the herbs over the noodles and add the tomatoes.
5. Add the beaten eggs and sprinkle the grated cheese over the top. Allow to cook in the pan for 3 - 4 minutes keeping the pan on a medium heat, this will allow the base of the omelette to brown slightly but the egg on the top may still be quite runny. Do not stir the omelette!
6. Put the frying pan, with the omelette in it, under a hot grill and brown the cheese and coo the top of the egg. Serve with salad.

VEGETABLE CURRY ★★

Preparation and cooking time 20 minutes   for 2

Vegetarian

You can add and take away vegetables from this recipe depending what you have to hand. Make sure that the vegetables which take longest to cook go in at the beginning, carrots and potatoes for example, mushrooms, cauliflower and broccoli types need to go in towards the end!

Oil to fry
2 cloves garlic, crushed
1 onion, chopped
1 courgette, sliced
14 oz/400g can chick peas
1 potato, cubed
4 mushrooms, sliced
veg stock cube

1 mug water
1 tablespoon tomato puree
1 oz sultanas
1 eating apple cut into medium chunks
2 tablespoons curry paste, depending on taste

Mint Raita
¼ pint yoghourt, creme frais or soured cream
1 tablespoon fresh mint or 2 teaspoons freeze dried

1. Fry the onion in the oil until soft.
2. Add the garlic, apple and potatoes, cook in the oil for 2 - 3 minutes.
3. Add the water and stock cube, bring to the boil and then simmer for 10 minutes.
4. Add the courgette, sultanas, mushrooms, tomato puree and curry paste. You may need to add a little more water. Cook for 5 minutes.
5. Add the chick peas and cook for 2 minutes.
6. Serve with rice.
7. To make the raita, just add the mint to the yoghourt, this will cook the curry down if you have put too much curry paste in! It also adds a good contrast to the flavour of the curry.

VEGETABLE STIR FRY ★

Preparation and cooking time 25 minutes   For 2

Vegetarian

Do not worry if you don't have a wok for frying, either a larger saucepan or your frying pan will work just as well. You can vary the vegetables used, remember to add the ones that need cooking the longest at stage 1.

Oil to fry
1 onion
1 small aubergine
1 courgette, sliced
4 mushrooms, sliced
1 clove garlic, crushed

14 oz/400g can chopped tomatoes
2 tablespoons soy sauce
1 tablespoon tomato puree
salt and pepper
1 teaspoon freeze dried basil
½ mug water or wine

1. Cut up the aubergine and fry with the onion in the oil.
2. Add the garlic, tin of tomatoes, soy sauce, the water or wine and cook for 5 minutes.
3. Add the courgette and mushrooms, soy sauce tomato puree and wine and cook for a further 10 minutes, stirring occasionally, add more water if necessary.
4. Add the basil, cook for 1 minute and serve with fresh crusty bread or toast.

Preparation and cooking time 15 minutes

for 1

This is a quick snack meal, has it's origins in Italy so you could always dream whilst your eating it! If you are vegetarian you could add tofu to this recipe.

1 teaspoon butter
½ onion, chopped
2 mushrooms
½ mug grated cheese
1 mug milk

1 desert spoon flour
2 slices cooked ham, cut into pieces
¼ teaspoon paprika
¼ teaspoon basil or chives, freeze dried
¼ mug pasta

1. Cook the pasta, see page 10.
2. Fry the onion in the butter.
3. Add the flour, stir well and cook for 30 seconds.
4. Add the milk, cheese and paprika and stir well. The mixture should thicken.
5. Add the ham and mushrooms and cook for one minute.
6. Drain the pasta and stir everything together.

Cooking and preparation time 20 minutes   for 1

If you like the mix of sweet and savoury this is a dish for you, refreshingly different and delicious.

2 teaspoons butter	1 egg
1 small onion, chopped	½ mug rice + ½ pilau rice cube
2 - 3 mushrooms, sliced	2 pineapple slices, cut into pieces.
1 tomato, cut into chunks	1 teaspoon soy sauce
1 slice of cooked ham, cut into pieces	1 teaspoon freeze dried coriander leaves
¼ red pepper, sliced	salt and pepper

1. Fry the onions in the butter until soft.
2. Add the mushrooms and peppers and cook for 30 seconds.
3. Add the cooked rice (see page 11), pineapple slices, soy sauce, ham and coriander leaves. Heat through gently.
4. Put a small amount of butter in a frying pan, beat the egg in a mug, put the pan on to heat. Once the butter is bubbling add the egg to it and allow it to spread thinly over the base of the pan. It will cook in less than a minute. Once cooked cut into strips and add to the mixture

MEATBALLS ★★★

Preparation and cooking time 20 - 25 minutes   for 2

This dish is a little fiddly but infinitely better than any meatballs you will buy in a tin!

Tomato Sauce
1 tablespoon oil to fry
14 oz/400g tin chopped tomatoes
2 tablespoons tomato puree
1 teaspoon freeze dried parsley or basil
1 onion chopped finely
1 clove garlic, crushed
1 teaspoon sugar
salt and pepper

Meatballs
½ x 500g pack of defrosted beef or lamb mince
1 egg
1 onion chopped finely
2 cloves garlic
salt and pepper

1. Make the sauce - fry the onions, add the rest of the ingredients and bring to the boil, simmer for 20 minutes.
2. Mix the mince, egg, garlic, onions and plenty of salt and pepper together in a bowl. Make into small balls, approximately 12 - 14.
3. Heat a little oil in a frying pan and cook the meatballs on medium heat. Turn them frequently, they will take approximately 10 minutes to cook through.
4. Check to see that they are cooked through by cutting one in half: if the meat is no longer pink in the middle they are done!
5. Serve with the tomato sauce and rice.

45

Preparation time 20 minutes, cooking time 30 - 35 minutes   for 2
Non vegetarian alternative!
The secret of good Toad in the hole is a hot oven and hot fat! Non vegetarians
may wish to replace all the vegetables with sausages!

Batter
1 mug plain flour
3 eggs, beaten
½ mug milk + 1 mug water
2 tablespoons white Flora or oil
pinch of salt

Butter to fry
1 clove garlic, crushed
1 onion, cut into chunks
2 carrots, sliced
6 - 8 green beans
few florets of broccoli
2 tomatoes cut into chunks
4 - 5 mushrooms cut in half
1 teaspoon freeze dried mixed herbs
salt and pepper.

1. Put the flour in the bowl and add the egg, salt and a little of the milk, mix well, beat with a whisk or a large spoon. Add enough milk and water to make the mixture look like single cream.
2. Put enough oil in the bottom of a large casserole dish or deep baking tray to cover the bottom. Put in a hot oven 220 C/Reg 9.
3. Boil the carrots and green beans in a little water , leave cooking while you fry the onions and the garlic. Add the broccoli to the cooking vegetables after 5 minutes or so.
4. Add the tomatoes, mixed herbs and cooked, drained carrots, beans and broccoli to the frying pan and stir, season with salt and pepper. Leave off the heat.
5. By now the fat should be very hot, it is best if it is smoking slightly. Carefully take out of the oven, pour the batter in, it should bubble around the edges as you pour it in. Carefully pour the vegetables on the top and spread them out.
If you are using sausages you do not need to cook them, just add them in raw, but they must be defrosted
6. Place the dish back in the oven, cook for 30 - 35 minutes or until browned. The mixture should rise around the edges. If the top of the 'toad' begins to get too browned before the centre is cooked turn down the temperature of the oven.

POTATO MASH ★★

Preparation time 5 minutes, cooking time 30 minutes   for 2
Vegetarian - with non vegetarian alternative

Butter to fry
1 small onion, chopped
1 carrot, sliced
6 - 8 green beans
2 potatoes, cubed
2 teaspoons flour
vegetable stock cube + ½ mug water
8 oz tofu (can add flaked tuna, pieces of ham, corned beef etc)
salt and pepper
1 teaspoon freeze dried parsley
2 teaspoons Worcestershire Sauce or HP sauce

1. Fry the onion, carrot, beans and potatoes, cook for 5 - 7 minutes to brown the
vegetables, season well.
2. Add the flour and cook for 1 minute
3. Add the stock cube and ½ mug water, together with the Worcestershire sauce.
4. Bring to the boil and then simmer for 15 minutes until the vegetables are tender.
5. Add the tofu or ham, corned beef or tuna and cook for 5 minutes.
6. Add the parsley and season well.

CHILI CON CARNE ★★

This is another standard dish which is useful to master, you can serve it with rice, pasta or crusty bread

1 teaspoon butter
1 large onion, chopped
½ x 500g pack frozen mince, either beef or lamb
2 cloves garlic, crushed
1 stock cube, beef or lamb
14oz/400g tin tomatoes
1 teaspoon chili powder, more if you like it hot
1 x 14oz/400g tin baked beans, you can use red kidney if you wish

1. Fry the onion in the oil until soft, add the crushed garlic.
2. Add the mince and cook until the meat is no longer pink.
3. Add the tin of tomatoes and the stock cube.
4. Add the chili powder and cook for 10 minutes
5. Whilst the chili is cooking put a potato in the microwave on full power for 5 - 6 minutes. If you do not have a microwave you will need to put the potato in the oven for 45 - 50 minutes, depending on the size. You obviously need to put the potato in before you start cooking the chili!
6. Add the beans to the chili and cook for a further one minute, taste to see if you would like more chili powder, if you add more cook for another one minute.
7. Serve with the baked potato or rice (see page 11).

QUICK SHEPHERDS PIE ★★

Preparation time 20 minutes, cooking time 25 minutes   for 2
vegetarian option

If you make enough for two this dish is ideal to reheat the next day.

½ x 500g pack of lamb, beef or Quorn mince
1 desert spoon gravy granules or Bisto
6 medium potatoes, cut into ½" cubes
1 mug water
salt and pepper
1 mug grated cheese
2 teaspoons butter

1. Put mince into a pan with the ½ mug water and bring to the boil, simmer for 10 - 15 minutes.
2. Put diced potatoes in pan with water, boil for 10 minutes and then drain. Add the butter and mix.
3. Add gravy powder to the meat, follow instructions on the packet of granules, differs according to brand. The gravy needs to be thickened to the consistency of double cream.
4. Pour mince into the bottom of a casserole dish.
5. Carefully spoon the potatoes on to the top, sprinkle with the cheese.
6. Cook for 20 - 25 mins at 180 C/Reg 7 until the top is browned.

Preparation time 15 minutes, cooking time 1 hour
for 2

Looks more complicated than it is. You must use chicken breast as legs and thighs will not cook in the time. This recipe gives a change of texture from the majority of sauce based dishes.

1 desert spoon milk
1 tablespoon mustard
½ mug grated cheese
1 and ½ tablespoons flour

1 teaspoon chopped chives
2 chicken breasts
2 large potatoes

1. Put potatoes on to bake, oven 200 C/Reg 8.
2. Mix milk and mustard together.
3. Mix together the grated cheese, flour and chives.
4. Dip the chicken breasts in the milk and then into the cheese mixture.
5. Place on a baking tray or the bottom of a casserole dish and pile the spare cheese on the top.
6. Bake in the oven with the potatoes for 30 - 35 minutes. The cheese should be browned when done.
7. Serve with salad.

CHICKEN CASSEROLE ★★

Preparation time 10 minutes, cooking time 1 hour
for 2

Quick and easy to prepare, leave it in the oven whilst you relax. If you want to use "cook in sauces" with chicken thighs follow this recipe to stage 2 but omit the flour and add the sauce.

4 chicken thighs
1 onion, chopped
4 - 5 mushrooms
2 cloves garlic
2 teaspoons flour

1 desert spoon cooking oil
14oz/400g tin tomatoes
2 teaspoons Worcestershire Sauce
1 teaspoon mixed herbs

1. Fry the chicken until brown on both sides, transfer into a casserole dish.
2. Fry the onions until soft, sprinkle the flour in and stir well.
3. Add the tin of tomatoes, garlic and herbs.
4. Bring to the boil and then transfer to the casserole, put a lid on and bake for 1 hour at 190 C/Reg 7.
5. Serve with rice or baked potatoes and green vegetables.

CHICKEN CURRY ★★

Preparation and cooking time 20 minutes   for 2

If you use chicken thighs in this recipe pre-cook them in the oven for 50 minutes in a casserole dish with a little water and salt and pepper. You can use left over cooked chicken or replace the chicken with mince, beef lamb or Quorn.

2 chicken breasts
1 onion, chopped
1 desert spoon cooking oil
2 teaspoons flour
3 cloves garlic, crushed
4 teaspoons mild curry paste (use less if the curry paste is hot)

1 potato cut into ½"cubes
1 mug water
1 chicken stock cube
½ mug natural yoghourt

1. Fry the onion and potato in the oil.
2. Cut the chicken breast into pieces and add to the pan. Cook for 2 - 3 minutes until the chicken is no longer pink on the outside.
3. Add the flour and stir well. Add the garlic, water, curry paste and stock cube, stir well.
4. Bring to the boil and then simmer for 10 - 15 minutes until the chicken and the vegetables are cooked.
5. Stir in the yoghourt but do not let it boil, cook gently for 1 minute.
6. Serve with rice (see page 11).

CREAMY CHICKEN ★★

Preparation and cooking time 20 minutes
for 1

This recipe is a little more expensive but is very easy to cook and delicious.

1 chicken breast, cut into pieces
½ onion, chopped
1 teaspoon butter
¼ pint double cream
½ teaspoon freeze dried basil

1 clove garlic, crushed
1 chicken stock cube
2 - 3 mushrooms
Rice to serve.

1. Put rice on to cook with ½ pilau rice cube (see page 11)
2. Fry onions in the butter until soft.
3. Add the chicken breast and the garlic, cook on a high heat until the outside of the chicken is no longer pink.
4. Add the cream and the stock cube, cook gently for 10 - 15 minutes, stirring occasionally.
5. Add the basil, cook for one minute.
5. Serve with rice.

Preparation time 20 minutes   for 2

This sweet and sour recipe can be used with a variety of things: meatballs, sausages, cooked beef or lamb and fish.

2 teaspoons butter
1 onion, chopped
2 chicken breasts cut into pieces
4 mushrooms, sliced
½ red pepper, sliced
1 clove garlic

Sweet and sour sauce
2 tablespoons tomato puree
3 tablespoons sugar
2 tablespoons white wine vinegar
1 tablespoon soy sauce
2 teaspoons cornflour
1 mug water

1. Put rice on to cook (see page 11)
2. To make the sauce, put all ingredients in a saucepan except cornflour and bring to boil.
3. Mix the cornflour with a little water, mix until smooth. Add to the boiling sauce, stirring well: it should thicken. Leave until chicken is cooked.
4. Fry onion mushrooms and pepper for one minute and then add chicken pieces, cook for 5 minutes.
5. Add the sweet and sour sauce and cook together for 2 minutes.
6. Serve with rice.

ROAST CHICKEN ★

Preparation time 5 minutes, cooking time 1 hour 25 minutes.

This recipe is for two people, if you just cook for yourself use less vegetables and the leftover chicken can be used the next day, either in sandwiches, risotto or pasta dishes.

1 onion
1 small chicken approximately 1.5 Kg.
3 potatoes
cooking oil.

1. Put oven on to 190 C/Reg 8.
2. Wash potatoes and cut into large pieces.
3. Peel the onion and cut into 6 wedges.
4. Remove any giblets from inside the chicken and place in an oiled flat roasting dish or a casserole. Add the potatoes and the onion and brush with oil. Cover with a lid or foil.
5. Cook for 1 hour, if you have a larger chicken then cook for longer.
6. Take the lid or foil from the chicken and cook for a further 25 minutes to allow everything to brown.
7. Serve with salad or vegetables.

CHICKEN DRUMSTICKS ★

Preparation time 5 - 10 minutes, cooking time 40 minutes
for 2

Look out for bargain offers in the supermarket, buy a quantity of drumsticks, if you want to use them in small amounts then separate them before you put them in your freezer. Larger quantities are useful for parties or just when you have a few friends around.

4 chicken legs
1 teaspoon mustard
2 teaspoon Worcestershire Sauce
½ teaspoon brown sugar
1 tablespoon tomato sauce
salt and pepper

1. Mix together the mustard, tomato sauce, Worcestershire sauce, salt, pepper and sugar.
2. Baste (spread over with a spoon) the chicken legs with half the liquid.
3. Place on an oiled baking tray or casserole dish. Bake for 20 minutes at 180 C/Reg 7.
4. Baste legs with the rest of the liquid and bake for another 20 minutes.
5. Serve with salad and bread rolls.

CHICKEN NOODLES ★★

Preparation time 10 minutes
for 1

This is nearly as quick as pot noodle but much more nutritious and tasty.

¼ x 250g pack of egg noodles
a little oil
one chicken breast or three small chicken fillets
2 spring onions sliced
½ chicken stock cube dissolved in ½ mug boiling water
1 teaspoon soy sauce
¼ red pepper
salt and pepper

1. Cover the noodles with boiling water and leave to stand for 4 minutes.
2. Cut the chicken into bite size pieces and fry in the oil.
3. Add the onion and pepper and fry for 2 minutes.
4. Add the stock and the soy sauce together with the drained noodles and cook for 1 minute.
6. Serve.

CHICKEN RISOTTO ★★

Preparation time 15 minutes, cooking time 15 minutes
for 1
This dish is great eaten cold, so you could double the quantity and eat half with
salad the next day.

1 chicken breast or 2 - 3 small chicken fillets
⅓ mug rice, can be risotto or basmati
¼ yellow pepper
2 mushrooms sliced
1 onion, chopped

½ teaspoon mild curry paste
½ chicken stock cube
¼ tin sweetcorn
1 mug water
1 teaspoon freeze dried chives

1. Fry the onion until soft.
2. Cut the chicken into bite sized pieces, add to the frying pan and fry for 2 - 3 minutes until the outside is no longer pink.
3. Add the mushroom and pepper.
4. Add the rice (uncooked), stock cube, curry paste and water, simmer gently for 20 minutes, stirring from time to time. Add more water if the mixture has dried up before the rice is cooked. There should be very little liquid left when the dish is finished.
5. Add the sweetcorn, heat through and serve.

CHICKEN HOT POT ★

Preparation time 5 minutes, cooking time 1 hour 30 minutes.

For 2

As you can see from the preparation time this recipe is very easy, you will have to wait for it to cook: just needs a bit of forward planning. You can add other flavourings to the stock, 2 teaspoons curry paste or 1 teaspoon chili paste. You can also replace the stock with a "cook in sauce" but you will need to add some water as the "cook in sauce" will dry up during the longer cooking time.

4 chicken thighs, skins removed.
2 mugs water
1 chicken stock cube
3 carrots, washed and sliced
3 large potatoes, washed and cut into chunks

1 onion, cut into 6 wedges
2 cloves garlic
salt and pepper

1. Put the stock cube in a mug, fill up with boiling water and stir until the cube has dissolved.
2. Put all the ingredients in a casserole dish, season with salt and pepper.
3. Pour the stock into the casserole.
4. Cover with a lid and cook for 1 hour 30 minutes at 190 C/Reg 8.
5. You can take the lid off for the last half hour to let things brown a little.

SPICY CHICKEN MEATBALLS ★★★

Preparation and cooking time 25 minutes   for 2

This dish is a little more difficult, try it after you have gained a bit of experience in cooking. You need to use fresh chilies, dried ones will not taste the same.

½ lb or 200g minced chicken
or 4 small fillets chopped
2 spring onions, chopped finely
1 small red chili, chopped finely
½ can sweetcorn
salt and pepper
oil to fry

Sweet and sour sauce
1 mug water
2 tablespoons tomato puree
3 tablespoons sugar
2 tablespoons white wine vinegar
1 tablespoon soy sauce
2 teaspoons cornflour.
rice to serve

1. To make the sauce - put all ingredients except the cornflour into a saucepan and bring to the boil. Mix the cornflour with a little water, add to the sauce: the mixture should thicken slightly. Leave until you have cooked the rest of the dish.
2. Put the rice on to cook (see page 11) whilst you make the meatballs.
3. Mix the thawed chicken, spring onions, chili, sweetcorn, salt and pepper together in a dish or bowl. Take care not to touch your face or eyes after chopping the chili, wash your hands well.
4. Put a little flour on a board or plate and make small balls from the meat mixture, use flour to stop the mixture sticking to your fingers.
5. Put a little oil in the frying pan and put the balls in, keep the heat at a medium level for 5 - 10 minutes. Turn the balls frequently, two forks will be the best tools for this.
6. Check to see if they are cooked by cutting through one of the meatballs: if the meat is no longer pink then they are ready.
7. Serve with rice and the sweet and sour sauce.

VEGETABLE BAKE ★★

Preparation time 15 minutes, cooking time 20 minutes.   for 2
vegetarian

You can use any mixture of vegetables for this dish: make sure that there are
some that you can fry at the beginning, as this gives more taste. Boil the
vegetables which take longer to cook, carrots, potatoes, parsnips etc.

1 desert spoon cooking oil
1 onion, chopped
1 carrot, sliced
1 courgette, sliced
4 mushrooms, sliced
1 sweet potato, cut into chunks
1/2 mug frozen peas

1/2 red or green pepper, sliced
small head of broccoli, broken into florets
2 x Quick cheese sauce (see page 19)
2 teaspoons Worcestershire sauce
salt and pepper
1/2 mug grated cheese

1. Place the carrots and sweet potato in a pan, cover with water and bring to the boil. Simmer
for 5 minutes and add the broccoli and peas, cook for another 5 minutes. Drain well.
2. Fry onions until soft, add mushrooms, peppers and courgettes, cook for 2 minutes.
3. Mix all the vegetables together, place in a casserole dish, sprinkle with the Worcestershire
sauce.
4. Make a double quantity of Quick Cheese Sauce and pour over the vegetables.
5. Sprinkle the grated cheese over the top and bake in the oven for 20 - 25 minutes
at 180 C/Reg 7. The cheese should be browned on top.

Preparation time 10 minutes, cooking time 10 minutes   for 2
vegetarian

The cauliflower and broccoli make a good combination of flavours. If you are not a vegetarian then you can serve this dish with crispy grilled bacon or sausages.

Quick Cheese Sauce
2 mugs grated cheese
3 desert spoons flour
2 teaspoons butter
2 mugs milk
¼ teaspoon paprika
salt and pepper

1 small cauliflower, broken into florets
1 small piece of broccoli, broken into florets
½ mug grated cheese.

1. Cook the cauliflower and broccoli for 5 - 7 minutes (see page 9)
2. To make the cheese sauce, put the grated cheese in a saucepan, add the flour and stir well. Add the milk, stirring well.
3. Put on a medium heat and bring to the boil, stirring well all the time. Once the sauce is thickened turn off the heat.
4. Put the drained vegetables in a casserole dish and pour the sauce over them, top with grated cheese, put under the grill to brown or in the oven at 200 C/Reg 8 for 10 - 15 minutes

CHEESY POTATOES★★

Preparation time 5 - 10 minutes, cooking time 35 minutes.
For 1   vegetarian

This is a useful recipe. You can eat the potatoes on their own or serve them with bacon, sausages, or some grilled fish. If you are vegetarian then serve with some green vegetables: broccoli or spring greens would work well. Cook the potatoes in a fairly large dish so that there is more surface area to brown on the top.

2 - 3 potatoes, cut into ¼" slices
1 x quantity of Quick Cheese Sauce (see page 19)
1 extra mug grated cheese
salt and pepper

1. Arrange the sliced potatoes in layers in the bottom of a small casserole dish.
2. Pour the cheese sauce over and season with salt and pepper.
3. Top with the grated cheeses
4. Bake in the oven at 180 C/Reg 7 for 30 - 35 minutes or until the potatoes are cooked and the cheese is browned.
5. Serve with bacon, sausages or salad.

CHEESE AND ONION ROSTI! ★★

Preparation and cooking time 20 minutes   for 2

vegetarian

This recipe makes a change to jacket potatoes. You can make Rosti with just potatoes, potatoes and onion, potatoes and cheese or add chopped tomatoes.

2 potatoes
1 onion
½ mug grated cheese
1 tablespoon freeze dried basil
oil to cook
1 teaspoon butter
tomatoes and spring onions to garnish

1. Grate the potatoes and onion and mix with the cheese.
2. Divide into two and form 'cakes'.
3. Heat the oil in the frying pan and cook on a moderate heat for 5 minutes each side.
4. Serve with salad.

SPICY VEGETABLE AND PASTA BAKE ★★

Preparation time 15 minutes, cooking time 25 minutes   For 2

vegetarian

If you like hot and spicy vegetarian food this is the dish for you. The vegetables can be varied. If you use things like potatoes and carrots you will need to boil them before adding to the mixture.

2 mugs uncooked pasta
1 tin Campbell's condensed cream of tomato soup, undiluted
1 tablespoon cooking oil   ½ red or green pepper. sliced
6 mushrooms, sliced   1 red chili, chopped finely
1 onion, chopped   1 teaspoon mixed herbs
2 courgettes, sliced   2 teaspoons Worcestershire Sauce
2 cloves garlic, crushed   1 mug grated cheese

1. Cook the pasta (see page 10).
2. Fry the onions until soft.
3. Add the mushrooms, courgettes, peppers, herbs and chili, cook for 2 minutes.
4. Add the tomato soup, bring to the boil and then take off the heat.
5. Drain the pasta and stir into the vegetable mixture.
6. Turn into a casserole dish and top with the grated cheese.
7. Cook for 25 minutes at 200 C/Reg 8 or until the cheese is browned.

Preparation time 10 minutes, cooking time 20 minutes   for 1 vegetarian

This dish is a tasty variation on the old macaroni cheese, it is quick to make and inexpensive.

1 x quantity of Quick Cheese Sauce (see page 19)

¾ mug pasta

1 tomato

1 egg

½ teaspoon mustard

1 teaspoon freeze dried chives

1 packet of crisps

½ mug grated cheese

1. Make the cheese sauce and leave to cool a little.
2. Cook the pasta (see page 10)
3. Beat the egg in a mug, add the chives and the mustard and mix with the cheese sauce.
4. Drain the pasta and put into a small casserole dish or oven proof bowl. Cut the tomato into 8 and mix with the pasta. Pour the sauce over the top.
5. Crush the crisps in the bag and mix with the grated cheese, sprinkle on the top of the pasta.
6. Bake at 180 C/Reg 7 for 20 minutes. The cheese and the crisps should be browned.
7. Serve with tomato or Worcestershire Sauce.

FISHERMAN'S PIE ★★★

Preparation time 20 minutes, cooking time 20 minutes.
For 2

This dish is slightly more complicated but worth the extra effort: fish does not reheat too well, so this is one best shared.

2 pieces frozen cod or haddock fillet (defrosted)
2 hard boiled eggs, each cut into 4
1 mug milk
2 teaspoons cornflour
5 medium potatoes, washed and diced
salt and pepper

½ mug grated cheese
1 teaspoon freeze dried parsley or basil
1 teaspoon butter

1. Place the milk and fish in the frying pan and simmer gently for approximately 5 minutes, or until the fish is white.
2. Mix the cornflour with a little milk and add to the pan, stir well, the sauce should thicken. Season with salt and pepper and gently break up the fish.
3. Add the hard boiled egg, mix gently and pour into a casserole dish.
4. Boil the diced potatoes for 8 - 10 minutes, drain off the water, add the butter and stir gently.
5. Place the potatoes on the top of the fish mixture and top with the grated cheese.
6. Cook for 20 minutes at 220 C/Reg 9, the top should be browned.
7. Serve with green vegetables or salad.

FISH IN CREAMY SAUCE ★★

Preparation time 15 - 20 minutes   for 1

This recipe is a little more pricey but healthy and quite easy to do. You can, of course, substitute pasta or rice for the potatoes.

1 Salmon Steak
½ - ⅓ cup pasta
a few green vegetables
¼ cup double cream
1 teaspoon freeze dried basil or parsley
Oil to fry
Salt and pepper
Potatoes, pasta or rice

1. Put potatoes on to boil, add the green vegetables to the pan after 7 - 8 minutes, they will then be cooked at the same time. If you use pasta add the green vegetables at the beginning, this means using only one pan!
2. Heat a little oil in the frying pan and cook the salmon steak. Use a high heat to seal each side first and then cook on a medium heat for approximately 10 minutes, depending on the size of the steak, if it is small and thin then it will only need 5 minutes.
3. Put the cream in a small pan and boil for about 1 minute, it will thicken slightly, add the basil or parsley.
4. Drain the pasta/potatoes and beans, add a little butter: serve with the fish and the sauce

TUNA AND PASTA BAKE ★

Preparation time 5 - 10 minutes, cooking time 20 minutes.
for 2 - 3

This is classic, very easy to cook food, inexpensive, quick and you can reheat the leftovers successfully. You can use different condensed soups, celery or chicken, for example.

1 tin Campbell's condensed cream of mushroom soup
1 can of tuna steak
2 mugs pasta
½ mug grated cheese
1 packet of crisps

1. Cook the pasta (see page 10).
2. Drain and place back in the saucepan, add the tuna and condensed soup (do not dilute the soup) mix well.
3. Transfer to a casserole dish.
4. Crush the crisps in the bag, mix with the grated cheese and sprinkle on top of the mixture in the casserole dish.
5. Cook for 20 minutes at 190 C/Reg 8 or until the cheese is browned.

TUNA AND RICE ★

Cooking and preparation time 10 - 15 minutes.
for 2

This recipe is extremely easy, you can use celery or chicken soup for variety and cook egg fried rice to accompany the dish, see page 11.

1 tin Campbell's condensed cream of mushroom soup
1 tin tuna steak
1 mug rice
2 mugs water
Salt and pepper

1. Put rice on to cook (see page 11)
2. Place the soup in the pan and heat, do not dilute as the tin suggests, bring to the boil.
3. Add the tuna and break up a little. Heat for 1 - 2 minutes. Season well with pepper.
4. Serve with the rice and some green vegetables, peas or beans. Season well.

FISHY PASTA BAKE ★★★

Preparation time 20 minutes, cooking time 20 minutes.

For 2

You can use different kinds of fish in this recipe: salmon, haddock, smoked haddock, trout. If you find fish on offer at the supermarket buy it and freeze ready to make dishes like this.

2 - 3 pieces of cod fillet (you can buy packets of frozen fillets)
1 small stem broccoli, broken into 'small trees'
2 spring onions
1 mug milk
½ mug frozen peas
1 teaspoon freeze dried parsley

1 mug pasta
2 teaspoon cornflour
Salt and pepper

1. Cook the pasta, broccoli and peas in the same pan for approximately 5 minutes, depending on the pasta you use.
2. Place the fish and the milk in a frying pan and cook gently for 4 - 5 minutes, remove the fish.
3. Mix the cornflower with a little milk and add to the hot milk in the pan, it should thicken.
4. Break up the fish gently and add to the thickened milk.
5. Drain the pasta and vegetables well. Add to the fish mixture, add the chopped spring onions and stir gently.
6. Pour into a casserole dish and top with the grated cheese. Cook for 20 minutes at 180 C/Reg 7. The cheese should be browned.

FISHY RICE ★★

Preparation and cooking time 15 minutes.
For 1
This recipe is based on the old Kedgeree dish, it is quite easy to do and makes a refreshing change from any fast food you may buy.

½ mug rice cooked with a pilau rice cube (see page 11)

1 piece smoked haddock
1 tablespoon milk
1 hard boiled egg
1 onion, chopped

1 teaspoon curry paste
1 - 2 mushrooms
½ teaspoon lemon juice
1 teaspoon freeze dried parsley or basil

1. Boil egg and peel, cut into 4.
3. Cook mushrooms and onion in a little butter in the frying pan, add the curry paste and mix. Take out of pan and leave to one side.
4. Put fish and milk in the frying pan and cook gently for 3 - 4 minutes, the fish should flake away from the skin when it is done.
5. Remove the fish skin from the pan and add the eggs, rice, mushrooms, lemon juice and parsley. Mix together and heat for 1 minute.
6. Can be eaten either hot or cold.

HOT POTATO SALAD ★★

Preparation time 15 minutes

for 2

This can be a meal in itself if served with green salad, or an accompaniment to a barbecue. It can be eaten hot or cold.

4 rashers of bacon	1 teaspoon freeze dried parsley
4 - 5 mushrooms	3 tablespoons olive oil
3 potatoes	1 teaspoon mustard
4 - 5 spring onions	1 tablespoon white wine vinegar

1. Cut the potatoes into medium sized chunks, boil for 10 minutes and drain.
2. Slice mushrooms and fry in a little oil until browned.
3. Fry bacon until brown and then cut into small pieces.
4. Mix the oil, mustard and white wine vinegar.
5. Mix all ingredients together, taking care not to break the potatoes up too much.

Preparation time 15 minutes
for 2

Makes a meal in itself with green salad or you can use it at barbecues or parties.

4 rashers bacon
2 hard boiled eggs
1 mug pasta
3 spring onions
3 mushrooms
2 tablespoons mayonnaise
1 tablespoon olive oil
Salt and pepper

1. Cook the pasta and the eggs in the same pan, add the eggs first and then the pasta a few minutes later so that it does not overcook: i.e. eggs for 10 minutes, then pasta and eggs for a further 5 minutes.
2. Fry the bacon until crisp and the sliced mushrooms until browned.
3. Chop the spring onions.
4. Mix the oil and mayonnaise together.
5. Drain the pasta and take the shells off the eggs. Cut the eggs into four.
6. Mix everything together and serve with a little green salad.

SALAMI SALAD ★★

Preparation time 15 minutes

for 2

This makes a lovely, refreshing summer meal. Salami is inexpensive but needs the right accompaniments to compliment it's strong taste.

Rocket or lettuce
1 tablespoon olive oil
8 slices salami
3 mushrooms
½ onion
¼ red pepper
2 tomatoes
3" cucumber

Dressing - you can make your own
or use a ready made vinaigrette dressing
Juice of ½ lemon
3 tablespoons olive oil
1 clove garlic, crushed
1 tablespoon white wine vinegar
1 tablespoon sugar

1. Fry the mushrooms, onion and pepper until browned: leave to cool.
2. Wash lettuce or rocket and spread over the plate.
3. Chop tomatoes and cucumber, add the salami, mushrooms, onion and pepper and arrange them on top of the rocket or lettuce.
4. Mix the dressing ingredients together and pour over the salad.
5. Eat straight away as the dressing will make the rocket and lettuce wilt and go brown.

COLD CHICKEN AND NUT SALAD ★

Preparation time 15 minutes   For 1

You can use left over chicken for this recipe. If you like the combination of sweet and savoury you will like this dish. There is also a contrast of textures: you can add other things to it such as spring onions, orange segments, peppers, mushrooms or cucumber.

Cooked chicken - either one chicken breast or 2 - 3 small chicken fillets
1 eating apple, Granny Smith or Golden Delicious
6 - 8 walnuts or pecans or ¼ mug cashews

¼ mug raisins   2 tablespoons creme frais
2 tablespoons mayonnaise   1 teaspoon freeze dried chives
2 celery sticks   Green Salad to serve

1. Cut the chicken into bite sized pieces.
2. Chop the celery into ½" pieces.
3. Cut the apple into small pieces, leaving the skin on.
4. Cut the walnuts or pecans in half, add the cashews whole.
5. Mix the mayonnaise and creme frais with the chives.
6. Mix everything together and serve with green salad.

Preparation and cooking time 10 - 15 minutes.
for 2

Any leftovers can be used in sandwiches the next day.

½ x 500g chicken mince or 2 chicken breasts cut into small pieces
1 red onion
1 teaspoon soy sauce
juice of ½ lime
1 clove garlic, crushed
1 teaspoon curry paste
2 teaspoons brown sugar
1 teaspoon freeze dried coriander
little oil to fry
Salt and pepper

1. Fry the onion in the oil until soft.
2. Add the mince and fry until the meat is no longer pink.
3. Add the rest of the ingredients, cook for 2 minutes and leave to cool.
4. Serve with salad.

Couscous Salad

Preparation time 10 minutes   for 1

You need to add plenty of tasty things to couscous plus some kind of dressing or sauce. It is very easy to prepare as you don't need to cook anything.

½ mug couscous
1 mug boiling water
1 tomato
2 spring onions
1" cucumber
1 teaspoon olive oil
juice of ½ lemon
1 clove garlic, crushed
1 teaspoon freeze dried chives
¼ red or green pepper chopped coarsely
1 tablespoon salad dressing or oil

Optional additions:
2 slices ham, cut into bite sized pieces
3 - 4 slices salami, cut into pieces
Prawns
Smoked mackerel or tuna broken into pieces

1. Put the couscous in a bowl and add the boiling water. Leave to stand for about 4 minutes. All the water should have been absorbed into the couscous, if not drain off the excess. Add 1 teaspoon butter and cook in a small pan on a medium heat for 1 minute. Leave to cool.
2. Chop the tomato, spring onion and pepper into small pieces.
3. Mix the salad dressing or oil, lemon, garlic and chives together.
4. Mix all the ingredients together including the optional additions and serve with a green salad.

RICE SALAD ★★

Preparation time 15 minutes   for 4

Vegetarian

This is an ideal accompaniment to barbecues, or can be eaten with cold meats, baked potatoes, potato wedges or green salads. Along with the basic ingredients in this recipe you could also add peppers, cucumber, gherkins, celery or raisins.

1 mug rice
Pilau rice cube
2 apples, Golden Delicious or Granny Smith
3 - 4 spring onions
½ tin sweetcorn
juice of ½ lemon
2 tablespoons olive oil
1 teaspoon freeze dried herbs

1. Cook the rice with the pilau rice cube (see page 11).
2. Chop the apple into small pieces.
3. Mix oil, lemon juice and chives together.
4. Chop spring onions and mix all the ingredients together.

TUNA SALAD ★★

Preparation time 10 - 15 minutes   for 2

This salad is great with barbecues or with cold meats, sausages etc. Again you can add other ingredients: cucumber, tomatoes or some curry paste to spice it up a little.

1 mug pasta
3 tablespoons mayonnaise or seafood dressing (100 Island)
½ tin tuna
1 mug frozen peas
4 - 5 spring onions
1 teaspoon freeze dried chives
Salt and pepper

1. Cook pasta and peas in the same pan. Drain and cool.
2. Chop onions.
3. Flake the tuna and mix all the ingredients together.
4. Serve with lettuce and tomatoes.

POTATO SALAD ★★

Preparation time 15 minutes
for 2
Vegetarian

Serve with cold meats and green salad. Ideal with barbecue food. You can add other things to this salad: peppers, cucumber, tomatoes, peas for example.

2 medium sized potatoes
4 - 5 spring onions
1 teaspoon freeze dried chives
1 teaspoon freeze dried mint
2 tablespoons creme frais
3 desert spoons Mayonnaise

1. Cut the potatoes into cubes and boil for 10 minutes.
2. Drain and leave to cool.
3. Mix the mayonnaise and creme frais together.
4. Chop the onions and mix everything together.

QUICK CHEESE CAKE ★★★

Preparation time 15 – 20 minutes.   Refrigeration time 4 hours.

for 4

250g packet of digestive biscuits
1/4 x 500g pack of butter
250g packet of cream cheese
10 fl oz / 1/2 pint double cream
2 tablespoons white sugar
rind and juice of a lemon
Fruit to decorate, e.g. oranges
or strawberries

1. Put the digestive biscuits into a polythene bag and crush them with a rolling pin, milk bottle or tin of beans. There should be no lumps left, just crumbs!
2. Melt the butter in a saucepan and add the crushed biscuit. Mix well.
3. Press the biscuit mixture into the bottom of a 20cm cake tin. If you do not have a cake tin use a small casserole dish.
4. Beat the cream and sugar together with a whisk until the cream thickens, don't keep beating once it has thickened or it will turn to butter.
5. Gently fold in the cream cheese, grated lemon rind and juice: the lemon juice is essential as it helps the cream to set. Pour on to the top of the biscuit mixture and gently spread out.
6. Leave in the fridge for 4 hours to set.
6. Decorate the top with fruit.

In order to get the cheesecake out of the tin you will need to use a cake tin with a loose bottom. Once the cheesecake has set, loosen the side with a knife and place the loose bottomed tin on a jam jar or tin and push the sides down. If you do not have an appropriate tin you can use a casserole dish but you will have to serve the cheesecake from it, don't try to get it out all in one piece!

Preparation time 5 minutes   For 4

This is a very quick and easy way of producing a dessert if you have friends around for a meal: keep the ingredients in your store cupboard! and the ice cream in your freezer drawer. You can add things on top of the chocolate sauce such as chopped nuts, 100's and 1000's, smarties, broken up flakes, small sweets etc.

125g = ¼ x 500g pack butter
3 heaped tablespoons Drinking Chocolate
4 heaped tablespoons sugar (brown or white)
2 tablespoons water

Buy the ice cream!

1. Place the butter, sugar and chocolate in a saucepan, heat and allow to boil for 1 minute.
2. Add the water, carefully, as it may spit at you! Boil for another 1 minute, stirring all the time. It should be smooth and thick by now.
3. Allow to cool slightly before serving on top of the ice cream. You will need to leave the sauce to cool longer if you are using glass dishes as the contrasts in temperature between the sauce and the ice cream may break thinner glass.

Preparation time 10 minutes, refrigeration time 2 - 3 hours.
For 4

Very easy to make and will impress your friends when you have them around
for a meal.

1 chocolate Swiss roll
1 tin raspberries
¼ mug sherry , brandy, Tia Maria or Cointreau
10 fl oz/ ½ pint double cream
2 tablespoon sugar
Cadbury's flake

1. Slice the Swiss roll into 1" pieces and arrange around the bottom of a dish: glass is preferable but a casserole dish will work just as well.
2. Pour the liquor evenly over the cake.
3. Put the raspberries and ½ the juice from the tin over the cake.
4. Whip the cream and sugar with a whisk until thickened, pour on the top.
5. Decorate the top with the broken up flake. Leave in the fridge for 2 - 3 hours until set.

Raspberries are the best fruit to use but you could also use apricots or pineapple, you will need to chop the fruit up a little.

FRUIT SALAD ★

Preparation time 10 - 15 minutes   for 2 - 3

Fruit salad is extremely easy to make: it will not last more than one day, as the fruits will begin to go brown. If you just have two or three fruits you can liven them up by making them into a salad. You can use a variety of fruits which could include the following.

Apples
Pears
Oranges
Bananas
grapes, seedless.
strawberries
Kiwi fruits
pineapple
peaches
nectarines
raspberries

for the juice
You can use either apple or orange pure fruit juice
If you prefer a more tangy fruit salad try the following:
1 lemon
1 orange
1 tablespoon sugar
¼ mug water

1. To make the juice, grate the rind of the lemon and the orange and squeeze the juices. Add the sugar and the water. Leave for the sugar to dissolve.
2. Cut the fruit into small pieces and mix together. If you use raspberries and strawberries add them at the end or they will break up in the mix and everything will be pink!
3. Serve with whipped cream.

CHOCOLATE CAKE ★★

Preparation time 10 - 15 minutes, cooking time 25 - 30 mins.

If you are a chocoholic this is an excellent recipe, you do not need a food processor; a cake tin is the best but you can cook it in a casserole dish!

⅓ x 500g tub of soft margarine or butter
¾ mug sugar
3 eggs
1 well packed mug self raising flour
3 tablespoons drinking chocolate
1 tablespoon water if required

1. Grease the cake tin well, a loose bottomed tin with a spring side is the best, but you could use a casserole dish. If you cut a round of greaseproof paper and put in the bottom of the cake tin, this will help the cake to come out after cooking. Put the oven on to heat up.
2. Put the butter and sugar in a bowl and beat with a wooden spoon.
3. Add the eggs, one at a time, and beat well.
4. Add the flour and the drinking chocolate: fold in gently with a metal spoon, do not beat the cake mixture at this stage. If the eggs you used were small and the mixture is very stiff add one tablespoon of water.
5. Pour the mixture into the tin and smooth out the top. Place in the oven at 170 C/Reg 6 for 25 - 30 minutes. When the cake is done you should be able to gently press it in the centre and it will not leave an indentation, but rather 'bounce' back a little.
6. Leave the cake to cool. Once cool cut the cake in half, horizontally.
7. You can fill the cake with fresh whipped cream in the middle and melt a bar of chocolate and spread it over the top of the cake; alternatively, you could make a quantity of chocolate sauce, boil it well, leave to cool and then pour over the top of the cake.

Preparation time 10 minutes, cooking time 20 minutes.   Makes 24

Muffins are very easy and inexpensive to make: the flavourings can be varied according to what you may have in the cupboards.

Basic recipe
3 mugs self raising flour
1 mug of brown sugar, you can use white.
2 eggs slightly beaten
1½ mugs milk
¾ mug vegetable oil

Variations
Chocolate chip muffins - add two 75g??? packets of chocolate chips, two different varieties work well, for example white and milk or plain chocolate. If you want double choc chip muffins instead of the 3 mugs of flour use 2 and ⅔ flour and ⅓ mug drinking chocolate.

Raspberry or blueberry muffins - take a 14oz tin of the fruit, drain the liquid from the fruit and add to the basic mixture.

Apple cinnamon muffins - add 1 mug of finely chopped apple to the mixture together with 2 teaspoons ground cinnamon.

Banana and nuts - add 1 mug of mashed, ripe banana plus 1 mug of chopped nuts, cashews, Brazils, pecans or walnuts work well.

Method

1. Mix all the ingredients together, they will be a bit lumpy and quite 'wet'.
2. If you do not have the individual cake tins, use your flat baking tray and arrange as many cake papers as you can on the tray, if you use them double they will hold their shape better. If you only have one baking tray the mixture will be ok if you leave it in the bowl whilst the first batch cook. Bake in the oven for 20 minutes at 180 C/Reg 7.

SCOTCH PANCAKES ★

Preparation and cooking time 15 minutes.

Scotch pancakes are really easy and inexpensive to make. You will usually have the ingredients in your cupboards, if not check to see if someone else has! They are great to make on a Sunday afternoon to eat whilst watching the TV or when friends drop in. Mixture makes approximately 16 small pancakes

I mug self raising flour
¼ mug brown sugar, can use white
2 eggs
¼ mug water
white flora or oil to fry.

1. Put everything but the water in a bowl and beat with a wooden spoon.
2. Add the water and beat well, the mixture is quite thick.
3. Heat a small amount of oil in the frying pan until it is quite hot.
4. Put 4 separate desert spoonfuls of the mixture in the hot pan and leave to cook for 1 minute. The mixture will rise slightly. Turn the pancakes over and cook on the other side for another minute, the pancakes will rise a little more.
5. Take out of the pan and eat immediately with butter and jam, maple syrup, ice cream etc.

Sample Menu and Shopping Lists

These menus and shopping lists assume that you have time to cook 3 or 4 times during the week and eat sandwiches and fruit for lunch each day and cereal or toast for breakfast.

Sample Weekly Menu and Shopping List 1

Monday	Cook Quick Shepherds Pie
Tuesday	Eat rest of Shepherds Pie
Wednesday	Baked Potato and grated cheese
Thursday	Eggie Bread and Beans
Friday	Cook Chicken Risotto
Saturday	Eat the rest of the chicken risotto
Sunday	Cook Noodle omelette and share it with a flat mate

Shopping List

Bread
Cereal
Milk
½ doz eggs
Butter or marg
Small bag potatoes
500g pack mince
block of cheese
1 tin beans
Fillings for sandwiches (see page 14)
Pack of small chicken fillets
1 yellow pepper
1 onion
fruit for lunches
few mushrooms
1 small tin sweetcorn

Check store cupboards for the following

Bisto or gravy granules
Rice
Curry paste
Chicken and beef stock cubes
Freeze dried chives
Salt and pepper

Sample Weekly Menu and Shopping List 2

Monday	Vegetable Soup, make enough for 2 days
Tuesday	Vegetable soup
Wednesday	Baked Potato with Tuna and Mayo, use the rest of the tuna in sandwiches the next day
Thursday	Chicken Casserole
Friday	Eat the rest of the Chicken Casserole
Saturday	Rosti and salad
Sunday	Beefy mince and pasta bake, share with someone.

Bread
Milk
Cereal
Butter
Eggs
1 small bag of potatoes
2 carrots
Salad
Garlic
Fruit for lunches
Celery, use for soup and eat the rest with your sandwiches
3 onions
Small pack frozen peas
Small jar mayo
1 x 14oz tin chopped tomatoes
Tin Campbell's condensed tomato soup
Tin tuna

Check cupboards for
Chicken stock cube
Flour
Worcestershire Sauce
mixed herbs
Rice
Pasta

Cheese
500g pack mince
4 chicken thighs
Ham, for sandwiches and the soup
Sandwich fillings

Sample weekly menu and shopping list 3

Monday	Spicy Risotto
Tuesday	Mince Hot Pot
Wednesday	Rest of Mince Hot Pot
Thursday	Roast Chicken and Potatoes
Friday	Use left over Chicken in omelette or with mayo and a baked potato
Saturday	Spaghetti Bolognese x 2
Sunday	Use left over Bolognese sauce, add curry paste and serve with rice

To buy
Bread
Butter
Milk
Cereal
Medium bag of potatoes
4 onions
10 mushrooms
garlic
Fruit for lunches
1kg pack of mince
Small frozen chicken to roast, approx 1.5 kg, take out of the freezer the night before.
2 x 14oz tins of chopped tomatoes
Sandwich fillings

Check cupboards for
Rice
Pilau rice cubes
Freeze dried coriander
Curry paste
Stock cubes
Tomato puree
Mayo
Oil to cook with

Monday   Beans on toast with poached or fried egg on top
Tuesday   Tuna and Pasta Bake
Wednesday Rest of Tuna and Pasta Bake
Thursday   Chicken and Sweetcorn Soup
Friday   Jacket Potato with cheese
Saturday   Pasta with Cheesy sauce and Ham
Sunday   Potato Hash

To buy
Milk
Cereal
Butter
Eggs
Bread
Cheese
2 mushrooms
2 onions
1 carrot
Few green beans
Bunch of spring onions
Fruit for lunches
Small bag of potatoes
1 tin beans
1 tin tuna
1 tin Campbell's condensed mushroom soup
Small tin of Sweetcorn
2 small chicken fillets
Ham
Tofu or tin of corned beef
Sandwich fillings

Check cupboards for
Pasta
Chicken stock cube
Soy sauce
Freeze dried chives
Worcestershire sauce
Flour

Sample Menu and Shopping List 5

Monday   Italian Soup
Tuesday   Scrambled egg on toast
Wednesday Spaghetti Bolognese, make enough Bolognese sauce for 2 days
Thursday   Use rest of Bolognese Sauce, add chili powder and serve with baked potato
Friday   Pasta with Tomato Sauce
Saturday   Chicken Curry
Sunday   Roast Potatoes and Sausages

Milk
Bread
Cereal
Eggs
Butter
Small bag of potatoes
1 carrot
4 onions
7 mushrooms
1 red pepper
Fruit for lunches
Celery, eat the excess with lunches
1 x 8oz tin of chopped tomatoes
2 x 14 oz tins tomatoes
1 tin beans
Frozen spinach
Packet of small macaroni

Check Cupboards for
Garlic
Chicken stock cube
Freeze Dried Basil
Tomato Puree
Spaghetti
Chili powder
Pasta
Oil for cooking
Curry paste

1 x 500g pack of mince
Ham for Friday and sandwiches
1 chicken breast or 2 small fillets
Small natural yoghurt
Sandwich fillings

Sample Weekly Menu and Shopping List 6

Monday   Lancashire Hot Pot
Tuesday   Rest of Lancashire Hot Pot
Wednesday   Omelette with crispy bacon and tomatoes
Thursday   Muligatawny Soup
Friday   Rest of Muligatawny Soup
Saturday   Chicken and Nut Salad
Sunday   Potato Wedges and Sausages

Check Cupboards for
Oil to cook with
Curry Paste
Chicken Stock cube
Rice
Garlic
Mayo
Freeze dried chives

To buy
Milk
Bread
Cereal
Butter
Eggs
3 onions
1 carrot
Celery
Lettuce
½ Cucumber
1 apple
Fresh tomatoes
Small bag of potatoes
Fruit for lunches

500g pack of cubed lamb or lamb mince
Cheese
Small carton of Creme Frais
Sausages
Small pack of bacon
4 small chicken breast fillets or 3 chicken breasts
Small packet of walnuts or pecans
Small packet of raisins
Sandwich fillings

Index